MATH ADVENTURES

SAM SOLVES

A WORD PROBLEMS ADVENTURE

by Elizabeth Everett
illustrated by Amy Zhing

Tools for Parents & Teachers

Grasshopper Books enhance imagination and introduce the earliest readers to fiction with fun storylines and illustrations. The easy-to-read text supports early reading experiences with repetitive sentence patterns and sight words.

Before Reading

- Discuss the cover illustration. What do readers see?
- Look at the picture glossary together. Discuss the words.

Read the Book

- Read the book to the child, or have him or her read independently.
- "Walk" through the book and look at the illustrations. Who is the main character? What is happening in the story?

After Reading

- Prompt the child to think more. Ask: Sam solves word problems by acting them out with objects and by drawing pictures. How do you solve word problems?

Grasshopper Books are published by Jump!
5357 Penn Avenue South
Minneapolis, MN 55419
www.jumplibrary.com

Library of Congress Cataloging-in-Publication Data

Names: Everett, Elizabeth, author. | Zhing, Amy, illustrator.
Title: Sam solves: a word problems adventure
by Elizabeth Everett; illustrated by Amy Zhing.
Description: Minneapolis, MN: Jump!, Inc., [2023]
Series: Math adventures
Includes index. | Audience: Ages 5–8
Identifiers: LCCN 2021970009 (print)
LCCN 2021058701 (ebook)
ISBN 9781636908700 (hardcover)
ISBN 9781636908717 (paperback)
ISBN 9781636908724 (ebook)
Subjects: LCSH: Word problems (Mathematics)
Juvenile literature.
Classification: LCC QA63 .E94 2023 (print)
LCC QA63 (ebook) | DDC 510—dc23/eng/20220126
LC record available at https://lccn.loc.gov/2021970009
LC ebook record available at https://lccn.loc.gov/2021970096

Editor: Jenna Gleisner
Direction and Layout: Molly Ballanger
Illustrator: Amy Zhing

Printed in the United States of America at
Corporate Graphics in North Mankato, Minnesota.

Table of Contents

How Many?

“Mom, can you help me solve word problems?” asks Sam.

"Sure!" his mom answers. "Read them to me. I will try to help."

"OK," says Sam. "The first problem is: *Josh has three apples. Nina has nine apples. Tess has four apples. How many apples are there total?*"

"I'm not sure where to start," says Sam.

"We will add them," says his mom. "Let's pretend these tomatoes are apples. We can use them to act out the problem."

Sam makes three groups of tomatoes.

1. Josh has three apples. Tess has four apples. Nina has nine apples. How many apples are there total? ____
2. A brown dog has five puppies. A white dog has three puppies. A black dog has five puppies. How many puppies are there total? ____
3. Noah's teacher has twenty cookies. There are sixteen students in the class. If each student eats one, how many cookies are left? ____

"How many tomatoes are there?" his mom asks.

Sam counts them.

"Sixteen!" says Sam.

"That's right! Counting them all tells you how many there are total," his mom explains.

3 + 9 + 4 = 16

"Thanks, Mom!" says Sam. "The second problem is: *A brown dog has five puppies. A white dog has three puppies. A black dog has five puppies. How many puppies are there total?*"

"I'll draw them!" says Sam.

"The total is thirteen puppies!" he says.

$$5 + 3 + 5 = 13$$

"Nice job!" his mom says. "You can solve this problem another way. Do you see where you can make ten?"

"Five plus five makes ten," Sam says. "And ten plus three is thirteen!"

$$10 + 3 = 13$$

"Third problem!" says Sam. "*Noah's teacher has twenty cookies. There are sixteen students in the class. If each student eats one, how many cookies are left?*"

"I want a cookie!" says Sam.

"Maybe for dessert," his mom says. "Now, how would you solve that problem?"

"I'll draw twenty cookies to start," says Sam.

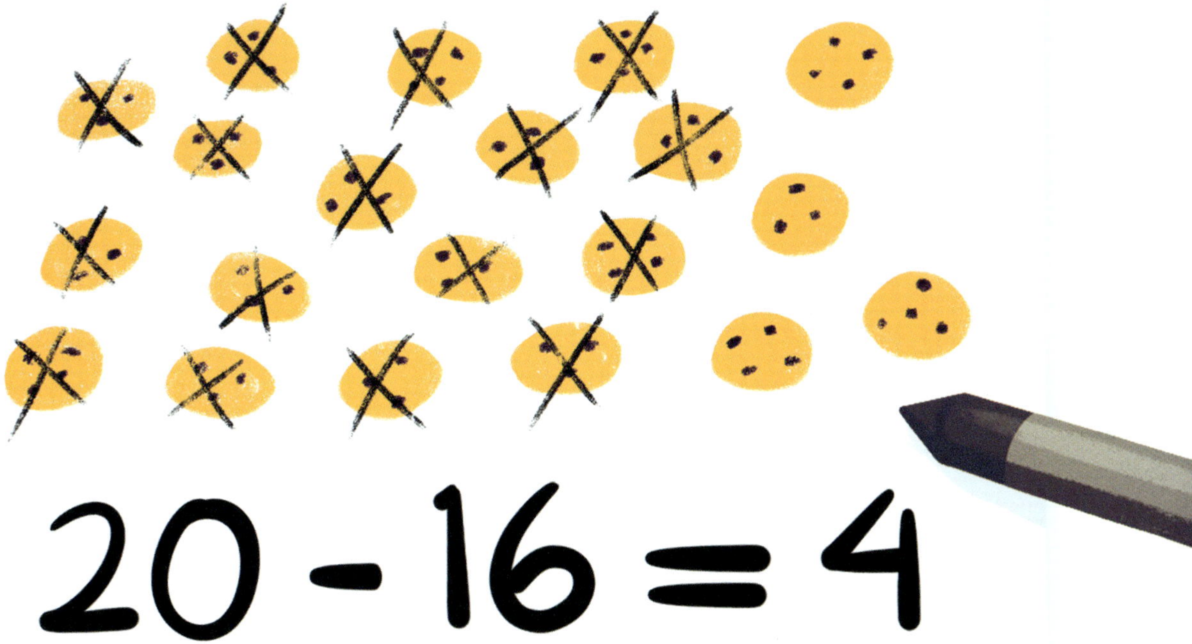

"Then I cross out sixteen to subtract. Twenty minus sixteen is four!" says Sam.

"Nice job, Sam!" his mom says. "How about we make cookies for dessert?"

How many apples are there total? 16
2. A brown dog has five puppies. A white dog has three puppies. A black dog has five puppies. How many puppies are there total? 13
3. Noah's teacher has twenty cookies. There are sixteen students in the class. If each student eats one, how many cookies are left? 4

Let's Review!

Sam draws and counts objects to solve word problems. Look at the word problems below. Can you count the objects to solve them?

1. Meg sees five trucks on the way to school. She sees five more at recess. On the way home from school, she sees two more trucks. How many trucks did Meg see today total?

2. After school, Meg plays outside. She sees three more trucks. Now, how many trucks did she see today total?

Let's Review! Answer Key: **1.** 12 **2.** 15

Picture Glossary

add
To find the sum of two or more numbers.

solve
To find an answer to a problem.

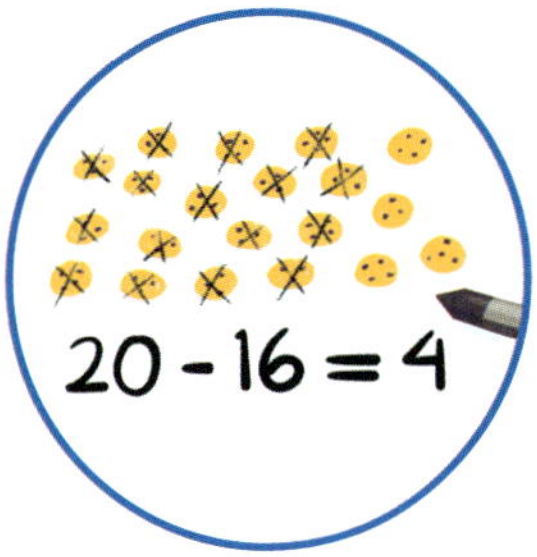

subtract
To take one number or amount away from another.

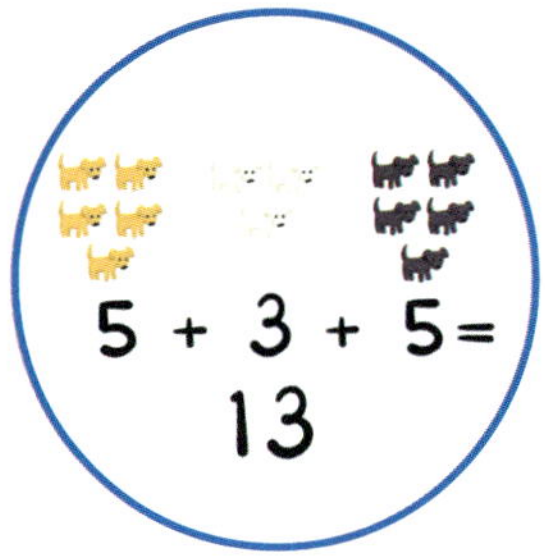

total
Making up the whole amount.

Index

To Learn More

FACT SURFER

Finding more information is as easy as 1, 2, 3.

1. Go to www.factsurfer.com
2. Enter "**Samsolves**" into the search box.
3. Choose your book to see a list of websites.

MATH ADVENTURES

LEVEL 2

Learn key math concepts you can use every day with these fun math storybooks. Have you read them all?

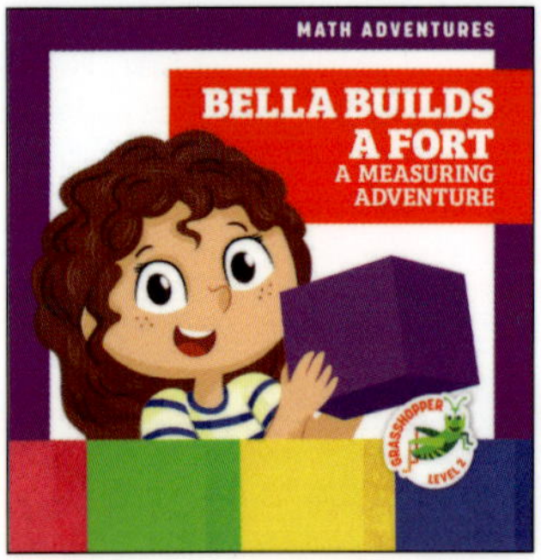

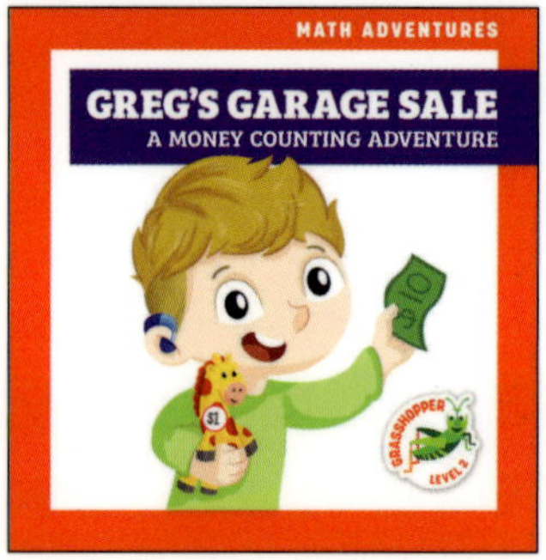

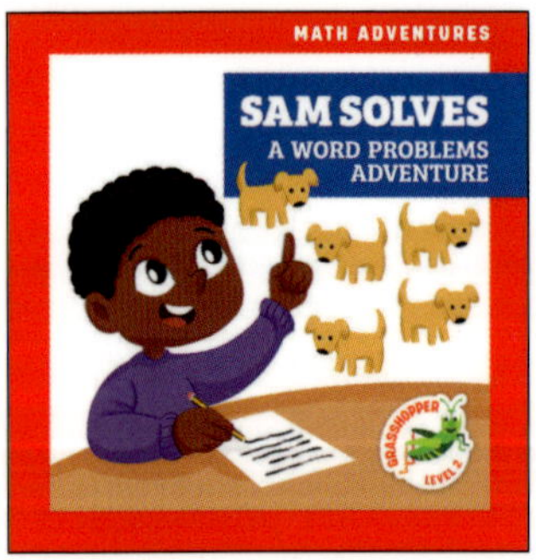

IL: Grades 1–2 GRL: H

ISBN 978-1-63690-871-7

www.jumplibrary.com
www.jumplibrary.com/teachers